To-Do List Formula

A Stress-Free Guide To
Creating To-Do Lists That Work!

Damon Zahariades

An ArtOfProductivity.com Action Guide

Other Productivity Action Guides by Damon Zahariades

The 30-Day Productivity Plan: Break The 30 Bad Habits That Are Sabotaging Your Time Management - One Day At A Time!
This action guide will help you to identify and break the bad habits that are preventing you from achieving your goals. Organized into 30 easy-to-read daily chapters, it's filled with hundreds of actionable tips.

* * *

Digital Detox: Unplug To Reclaim Your Life
Stress levels are rising. Relationships are suffering. Our phones and other devices are largely to blame. Digital Detox provides a step-by-step blueprint for people who want to take a break from technology and enjoy life unplugged.

* * *

The Time Chunking Method: A 10-Step Action Plan For Increasing Your Productivity
The Time Chunking Method is one of the most popular time management strategies in use today. If you struggle with getting things done, you need this action guide. Productivity experts around the world attest to the method's effectiveness!

* * *

To-Do List Formula: A Stress-Free Guide To Creating To-Do Lists That Work!
Most people use to-do lists that hamper their productivity and leave them with unfinished tasks. This action guide highlights the reasons and shows you how to create effective to-do lists that guarantee you get your important work done!

For a complete list, please visit
http://artofproductivity.com/my-books/

Your Free Gift

I have something for you. It won't cost you a dime. It's a 40-page PDF guide titled *Catapult Your Productivity! The Top 10 Habits You Must Develop To Get More Things Done.* I'd like you to have a free copy with my compliments.

You can grab your copy by clicking on the following link and joining my mailing list:

http://artofproductivity.com/free-gift/

Before we jump into *To-Do List Formula: A Stress-Free Guide To Creating To-Do Lists That Work!*, I'd like to express my thanks. I realize there are many books on this subject that you could otherwise spend your time reading. You're taking a chance on me. I appreciate it. Giving you a free PDF copy of my guide *Catapult Your Productivity* is my way of showing that appreciation.

On that note, let's dig in. You're going to love what's coming your way in the following pages.

Contents

Foreword

The to-do list is one of the simplest task management systems in use today. Yet it continues to frustrate millions of people. You may be one of them.

First, it's not your fault. Few people receive formal training on how to create effective to-do lists. It's rarely taught in school. And by the time most of us enter the workplace, we've adopted a poor, ineffective approach to getting things done.

Second, without solid training, you're likely using a task management method that's sabotaging your ability to complete tasks. I call this the "productivity paradox," which we'll discuss in detail in a few moments.

The results are catastrophic.

Without a proper strategy to manage tasks, our days spiral out of control. Our stress levels skyrocket as high-priority items linger past their deadlines. Meanwhile, a constant stream of new tasks comes in and demands our attention. We begin to feel overwhelmed as our to-do lists grow past the point where we can reasonably expect to get everything done.

That's life for millions of people.

It's the reason I wrote this action guide, *To-Do List Formula: A Stress-Free Guide To Creating To-Do Lists That Work!* I'm going to show you how to manage tasks and create to-do lists that help you to get your important work done. This single skill will cause much of the stress you're feeling to evaporate.

To-Do List Formula is a short book designed to help you take action as quickly as possible. That's important. You're reading it because you feel swamped, buried under a mountain of tasks, projects, and responsibilities. The system I'm going to outline for you will show you how to regain control of your workday and stay ahead of the curve.

This action guide isn't meant to be skimmed and shelved. It's meant to be read and applied. The good news is that the material has been written and organized in a way that makes it easy to read through it quickly. You can also choose to read only the sections you feel are important to you.

Application of the material is up to you.

The title of this book, *To-Do List Formula*, shouldn't be taken to imply that a single, perfect task management approach will work for everyone. On the contrary, the goal is to identify the approach that best complements your personal work process.

To that end, I'll describe several to-do list systems in use today. Each one has useful features as well as noteworthy flaws. After we discuss these systems, I'll show you how to create effective lists. I'll take you through the process, step by step.

Toward the end of this action guide we'll talk about how to keep the machine well-oiled so it continues to work flawlessly for you day after day. I encourage you to adopt the tactics that work for you and abandon the rest.

As I've highlighted in my other books, you're the captain of your ship. I'll provide the map and make actionable recommendations. You plot the course.

One last note...don't be intimidated by this book's table of contents. I've organized this material so you can easily find the sections that will deliver the greatest impact in your life. You don't have to read them all if you don't want to. Read the ones that interest you now and save the others for later.

Having said that, if you're feeling completely overwhelmed, I recommend you read this action guide from beginning to end. You'll learn why your current approach to task management is failing. You'll also discover the changes you need to make to meet your deadlines, lower your stress, and find more joy in your daily experience.

By the time you finish reading *To-Do List Formula: A Stress-Free Guide To Creating To-Do Lists That Work!*, you'll know how to create task lists that do more than just display action items. They'll actually help you to get things done. More to the point, they'll help you to get the *important* things done. That could mean the difference between struggling with chronic stress and self-guilt and enjoying a relaxed, pressure-free workweek.

You're about to learn a system that will revolutionize how you approach your work, both at the office and at home.

Ready to get started? If so, let's jump in.

What Are Your To-Do Lists Supposed To Accomplish?

Here's what a solid to-do list strategy will do for you:

First, it will give you control over your workday. You'll know what you need to work on and what can be put on the back burner. A good task management system will make your workday less chaotic.

Second, you'll be able to meet your deadlines. A solid to-do list will reveal the day's top priorities based on their importance and urgency. It will show you instantly where you should devote your time and attention.

Third, your to-do list will ensure you're working on the right tasks at the right time. Accordingly, you'll get urgent items done and be able to focus on less-urgent items as time permits. Rather than feeling overwhelmed, you'll feel like you're ahead of the curve.

Fourth, you'll avoid wasting valuable time putting out fires. Remember, your task list will show you what you need to work on based on each item's urgency. You'll learn to rely on it to manage your time. A proper list will prevent you from reacting to events that seem like crises. Instead, you'll assess each situation based on your current workload, and make rational decisions regarding where you should spend your limited time.

It's worth noting that few "crises" are true emergencies. They only seem so when we react to them emotionally. You probably know this from experience. Your task list removes the emotion so you can make good decisions that maximize your productivity.

Speaking of productivity, a proper to-do list will help you to get more done in less time. Importantly, you'll get the *right* things done. Remember, being productive isn't about completing a long list of tasks. It's not about staying busy. It's about focusing on high-value activities that help you to accomplish your goals.

Sixth, your task list will greatly reduce your stress. You'll be able to meet your deadlines, and thus won't experience the constant, unpleasant, creativity-killing pressure that accompanies completing tasks late. You'll avoid being distracted by supposed crises, which will make you feel more in control of your workday. You'll concentrate on high-value tasks, which ensures you'll spend your time in the most efficient manner possible.

Seventh, a properly designed to-do list will improve your focus. When it comes to getting things done, focus is where the battle is won. As noted above, your list will show you where to spend your time. You'll know which tasks carry a higher priority than others, and thus deserve your immediate time and attention. Focus is what allows you to get important work done rather than waste time on minor or trivial activities.

Lastly, a good task list will eliminate the frustration and guilt you feel when you fall behind on projects. It will help you to work more smartly and with greater purpose. You'll focus on items that move you closer to your goals, giving you a real sense of accomplishment at the end of each day.

In the next section, we'll talk about how your current to-do lists are preventing you from getting things done. I call this the Productivity Paradox.

The Productivity Paradox: How Your To-Do Lists Are Hampering Your Success

Take a look at the following numbers, courtesy of productivity app developer iDoneThis.

- 41% of to-do items are never completed.
- 50% of completed to-do items are done within a day.
- 18% of completed to-do items are done within an hour.
- 10% of completed to-do items are done within a minute.

What do these numbers tell us? First, they reveal that many to-do lists are ineffective. Specifically, the task management systems *behind* the lists are ineffective. After all, more than 40% of tasks are never finished. The implication is that the items are carried over to the following day, postponed indefinitely, or dropped altogether. These are not the signs of an effective task management system.

Second, many to-do list items are completed quickly, some within minutes. This suggests many people's lists fail to specify the amount of time individual tasks will take to complete. It also demonstrates that people tend to pick tasks that appear easy to do. The problem with this approach is that it fails to address task priority. A large number of to-do items may get crossed off the list, but there's no indication they're the *right* items - the important stuff. This gives the individual a false sense of accomplishment.

Third, it indicates that many to-do lists are too long. They're overloaded with tasks. This causes us stress since we know we'll never be able to address every item on our lists. We'll be forced to carry them forward or abandon them.

Data suggests most of us won't even get close to completing every item on our to-do lists. According to iDoneThis, 41% of our to-do items will routinely remain unfinished. This problem is more prevalent than most people imagine. According to a survey by LinkedIn, nearly 90% of professionals admit to not getting through their task lists on a regular basis.

Fourth, the data above suggest that many people approach task management without having a clear grasp of their schedules and availability. Again, consider that 41% of tasks go unfinished. This is a disturbingly high number if we're measuring our productivity by task completion.

The above describes the Productivity Paradox. We create to-do lists to help us organize tasks, manage our time, and get things done. But because we rely on ill-conceived task management systems, we inadvertently create lists that sabotage our efforts.

In doing so, we forfeit our productivity. We end up getting less done instead of more.

In the next section, we're going to take a close look at your current to-do list system. Unless you've received formal task management training, there's a fair chance your lists are hampering your success.

Why You're Not Finishing Your List Of To-Do Items

Ideally, you should be able to cross off every item that appears on your to-do lists at the end of each day. If you're having difficulty doing that, carefully read this section.

I'm going to cover the eight most common reasons people fail to get through their lists. Any one of them can wreck your productivity and prevent you from getting things done on time.

Reason #1: You Misunderstand The Goal Of To-Do Lists

Why do you create to-do lists? What do you hope to accomplish with them?

Most people answer "to get things done." But that's not the purpose of a properly designed to-do list.

The main purpose of your to-do list is to help you organize your tasks and projects, and highlight the important stuff. It allows you to get everything out of your head, where things are likely to fall through the cracks. By writing them down, you'll collect them in one place and gain a bird's-eye view of your biggest priorities.

A list of items displayed in front of you is much easier to manage than the same list swimming around in your head. You can more easily organize tasks according to when they need to be completed and plan your day accordingly. This alone will help you to focus on your most important work.

Most people misunderstand the function of a to-do list. They believe it's a tool that should help them to complete every task they think deserves their attention. On the contrary, a solid to-do list will focus your attention on the right work and prevent you from getting sidelined by less-critical items.

Your task list isn't a tool for getting everything done. Rather, it's a tool that will ensure you get the *right* things done.

It's important to understand the difference. If you misinterpret the purpose of your to-do lists, you'll end up creating and using them ineffectively. That, in turn, will guarantee that your lists hamper your productivity rather than increase it.

Later in this action guide, I'll show you precisely how to create lists that works to your benefit. You'll want to modify my system to accommodate your work flow and personal preferences, of course. But you'll find the basic principles that underpin a solid to-do list system are universally applicable.

Reason #2: You Neglect To Assign Deadlines

A to-do list without deadlines is a wish list. Nothing more. Without deadlines, we lean toward inaction.

Deadlines do more than just impose a sense of urgency. They help us to prioritize tasks and projects based on the amount of time we have to complete them. Additionally, when they loom, they spur us to take action.

Consider this: how quickly would you pay your credit card bill if there was no due date for the payment? How quickly would you pay your car registration? If you're like most people, you'd postpone both tasks indefinitely.

This same outcome occurs when people create to-do lists and neglect to assign a deadline to each task. Without deadlines, there's little impetus to act. Without an impetus, nothing gets done. This is the reason so many to-do lists spiral out of control, growing longer and longer by the day as tasks go unfinished.

This is a major problem because most people struggle with procrastination. Even those of us who have managed to curb the habit must be ever-vigilant lest it rears its head and regains a foothold in our lives.

Deadlines are the enemy of procrastination. They motivate us to take action and finish tasks. They also help us to gauge the effectiveness of our time management efforts. If we're consistently getting important things done on time, we must be doing something right.

Deadlines also help us to decide where to spend our limited time and attention. This is important. There will always be more tasks to finish than the time needed to finish them. Deadlines help us to choose between competing tasks based on the goals we hope to accomplish.

Recall Parkinson's Law: "Work expands so as to fill the time available for its completion." If you choose not to assign deadlines to your to-do items, don't be surprised when those items linger on your list.

Reason #3: Your Lists Are Too Long

You know what I'm referring to. I'm talking about daily task lists that seem to never end. They go on and on, containing dozens of items.

Such lists are counterproductive in a number of ways. First, they're distracting. They present too many options, each of which pulls your attention away from your most important work.

Second, they're unrealistic. Lists that are too long eventually reach a point at which they become unmanageable. You're unable to get to every item because there are simply too many of them.

Third, they're discouraging. You finish each day realizing that you failed to complete the day's list of tasks. This outcome, experienced over and over, can be devastating to your motivation.

Fourth, they encourage procrastination. By failing to complete your to-do items day after day, you train your mind to accept that outcome. With time, you'll lose the drive, or impetus, to complete tasks in a timely manner.

You have a limited amount of time to get things done during the course of a given day. It follows that you should limit the scope of your to-do list to accommodate this constraint. If you only have four hours at your disposal, make sure the items on your to-do list can be completed within that time frame. Otherwise, you'll set yourself up for failure.

Many people do a brain dump of every task they need or want to get done. They record everything on a single list. The problem is, they neglect to categorize these tasks and put them on separate lists according to context, priority, and urgency. The items remain on a single massive register, which is then referred to each day as a rolling reminder of what needs to get done.

This is a terrible approach to task management. It results in a long list that grows longer as new tasks are added each day.

Reason #4: Your Lists Have Too Much Variability

To-do lists that serve as brain dump repositories invariably collect tasks that vary too broadly in scope. Items that will take three minutes to complete are listed next to items that will take three *weeks*. High-priority tasks are listed next to low-priority tasks that can be put on the back burner indefinitely. You'll also find items associated with a wide swath of unrelated projects.

In other words, there's no connection between the various tasks.

There are serious consequences to this approach. First, faced with a long list of options, you're likely to either become paralyzed with inaction or spurred to engage in a low-value activity, such as checking Facebook. This is what psychologist Barry Schwartz called the "Paradox of Choice." The more options we have, the less capable we are to decide between them and the more anxiety we experience as a result.

A second consequence of having too much variability in your task lists is that you take longer to get things done. Whether you're paralyzed with indecision or off checking Facebook as a way to avoid choosing between your many options, you ultimately waste valuable time. That hurts your productivity.

Third, too much variability in your to-do lists increases your stress levels. You're more distracted, which means you'll work less efficiently. You're unable to choose which task you should work on, which destroys your ability to manage your time. Consequently, you're left with less time to complete important projects, which forces you to work harder to get things done on deadline. With less time available, you're more likely to miss deadlines, which can trigger feelings of guilt, shame, and frustration.

These circumstances can cause your stress levels to skyrocket. That, in turn, will make it more difficult to produce high-quality work you can be proud of, and do so on time.

The good news is that you can easily avoid the above problems once you know how to create effective to-do lists. I'm going to show you the steps later in this action guide.

Reason #5: You Give Yourself Too Many Options

This issue is closely related to having too much variability in your task lists. But it deserves its own mention due to its effect on how the brain makes decisions.

We wake up in the morning with a limited store of cognitive resources. This store is quickly used up throughout the day as we make decisions. All decisions, simple and complex, take a toll.

This is the reason it's easy to choose between multiple options in the morning - for example, should you have waffles, eggs, or cereal for breakfast? You have a full store of cognitive resources at your disposal. At the end of the day, however, even the simplest of choices can seem difficult. Should you go to the gym, watch television, or have a meaningful conversation with your spouse? You're tired and have fewer cognitive resources at your disposal. As a result, your ability to make rational decisions is impaired.

This is called decision fatigue. It's a state in which you're less able to make good decisions because you're mentally exhausted from making decisions throughout the day. In other words, your cognitive resources have been exhausted. You're running on fumes.

This phenomenon is important to understand because it has a disastrous effect on our ability to decide how to allocate our time between competing options. We become less rational, less focused, and less able to control our impulses. Consequently, we're more inclined to choose activities that offer immediate gratification over those that are arguably better for us, but require more effort.

For example, at the end of the day, suffering from decision fatigue, we're more likely to watch television than go to the gym. We're more likely to grab a bag of potato chips than prepare a salad or cook a steak. We're inclined to choose the easy path.

To-do lists that present too many options exacerbate this

problem. They force you to make unnecessary decisions concerning which tasks to work on. As mentioned above, each decision erodes your store of cognitive resources and increases your decision fatigue.

This eventually leads to a predicament known as "decision avoidance." Confronted with too many options, you avoid picking from among them because doing so requires too much mental effort. Instead, you spend valuable time checking email, visiting Facebook, and reading news headlines, all in an attempt to sidestep the act of deciding what to work on.

The result is predictable. Your productivity plummets and your to-do items, including the important ones, go unfinished.

Reason #6: You Neglect To Add Context For Each Task

One of the greatest failings in most to-do lists is a lack of context for individual tasks. Items are written down without any indication about the time needed to complete them, their priority, and the roles they play in achieving specific goals.

Without such context, it's difficult to know which tasks deserve your immediate attention. In fact, it's difficult to even know if you're able to work on a particular task given your circumstances.

If you don't know how long something will take to finish, how important it is, and how it contributes to your goals, how can you know whether you should work on it? If you don't know whether you need access to certain resources to work on the task, how can you know whether working on it is even possible at a particular point in time?

The answer is, you can't know.

This is the reason to-do lists that offer no task-level context are ineffective. In fact, they do more harm than good. Rather than prompting you to work on your most important tasks, they cause you to waste time on items poorly-suited for your current circumstances.

For example, suppose your to-do list includes the task "call my accountant." It provides no information about the item's priority. Do you need to call your accountant today or can it wait until next week? Nor is there any information concerning how long the call is likely to last. Will it take a few minutes or will you be on the phone for an hour? Also lacking are details regarding the purpose of the call. Do you need to ask your accountant a question about a potential write-off? Or do you want to explore the pros and cons of starting a shell corporation?

The point is, it's difficult to know whether you should tackle a to-do item without knowing its contextual details.

When you create a list of tasks without context, you end up with options that are difficult to choose from. The result? Your list, which is supposed to be a record of things you need to get done, becomes a growing record of things left unaddressed and unfinished.

Reason #7: Your Tasks Are Defined Too Broadly

The problem with broadly-defined tasks is that they're too large in scope. Many lack a clear starting point and ending point. As a result, there's no way to properly measure success.

For example, suppose one of the items on your to-do list is to "build a website." This task is too broadly defined. Building a website involves several steps, many of which cannot be executed until others are completed. You would need to reserve a domain name, find a web host, create a hosting account, point your nameservers to the host's servers, install Wordpress, install a theme, install Wordpress plugins, and much more.

In other words, this broadly defined to-do item is actually a full-blown project made up of numerous tasks.

If this item were on my to-do list, I wouldn't know how to get started since I neglected to list the individual tasks. I would be inclined to procrastinate. That being the case, it would remain on my to-do list unaddressed, causing me anxiety that increases each day as I fail to make progress on it.

In contrast, a *narrowly*-defined task implies clear starting and ending points. For example, you'd know when the task "reserve a domain name" has been completed. You'd know when the task "find a web host" has been completed. These to-do items carry a singular objective, and it's easy to know whether that objective has been met.

Projects masquerade as tasks when they haven't been broken down to their constituent parts. Because the individual to-do items are left unspecified, it's difficult to know when the projects have been completed.

This is a common failing in to-do lists.

For example, consider an author who intends to write a new novel. The to-do item "start writing novel" is too vague. There are too many tasks involved that are left unspecified. "Write the first draft of Chapter 1" would be more effective. Its specificity encourages action and makes it easy to know when the item has been completed.

Consider a college student who needs to prepare for an exam. The to-do item "study for exam" is imprecise. "Complete practice problems on pages 171 - 175" would be more effective as it gives the student a specific task to address.

Consider a corporate manager who wants to improve his department's workflow. The to-do item "increase department productivity" is ambiguous. "Schedule meeting with team leaders to discuss new workflow plan" would be more effective since it presents a single objective. It's easy to know when that objective has been met.

The point is, defining tasks too broadly is detrimental to their completion. Their vagueness ensures they linger. If you're having trouble completing to-do items, check whether they can be broken down to smaller tasks.

Reason #8: Your Tasks Are Not Attached To Specific Goals

Everything you do has a purpose. For example, you change the oil in your car to keep the engine in good shape. You file your income taxes on time to avoid penalties and fines. You make a reservation at your favorite restaurant to avoid having to wait 45 minutes for a table.

Our goals spur us to take action. We're less inclined to procrastinate when we're able to predict the positive result of completing a specific task. All other variables being equal, the more certain we are of the outcome, the greater the likelihood we'll act.

Strangely, many people forget this principle when creating their to-do lists. They write down (or record online) every task that comes to mind. But they fail to associate these tasks with specific goals. Consequently, they end up spending their limited time working on to-do items that matter little to them in the long run.

For example, suppose you maintain a blog and record "write a new blog post" on tomorrow's to-do list. It's a task you assume you need to do. But do you know the specific reason you need to do it? Are you trying to achieve a particular goal with the new blog post?

Perhaps you hope the new post will receive exposure on Facebook and Twitter, resulting in an influx of traffic to your website. Maybe you want to give Google another reason to display your blog on its first page of listings for popular search queries. Or perhaps you hope your blog post will gain the attention of influencers in your industry.

That can set the stage for making valuable connections and propel you to the position of a thought leader.

The point is that you must attach a specific goal to each task on your to-do list. Know the reason each item needs to be completed. If you neglect this step, you'll be less motivated to get the item done.

You may relate to this from experience. If so, don't despair. I promised to show you how to create to-do lists that spur you to take action, help you to work more efficiently, and increase your productivity. I'll make good on that promise in upcoming sections.

Before we get there, though, let's do a quick self-appraisal of your to-do list proficiency.

Assessing Your To-Do List Mastery: A Self-Appraisal

Before I show you how to create task lists that work, it's worth evaluating the effectiveness of your current lists. It's not enough to know that you never complete them. You should have a good idea concerning the reasons.

To that end, the following questionnaire will help you to assess your to-do list proficiency. It will reveal your strengths along with the facets of task management that may need attention.

It's quick and easy. Simply answer each of the following eight questions, giving yourself a score between one and five. A score of one signifies that you need help and a score of five signifies that you're proficient. (You'll note that each of the eight questions below corresponds to the eight reasons we just covered concerning why you're not getting through your daily list of to-do items.)

Tally your points after you answer the questions and find out how skilled you truly are at creating effective to-do lists!

1. Do you understand the primary role to-do lists serve in a task management system?

2. Do you assign deadlines - a specific date rather than "by the end of the month" - to each to-do item?

3. Do you limit the number of items on your to-do lists to 10? (If so, give yourself three points.) Do you limit the number to seven? (If so, give yourself five points.)

4. Do you create your to-do lists with minimal variability? Focus on the time needed to complete each task as well as each task's priority. For example, do you have 3-minute tasks listed with tasks that will take 3 hours? Do you have A-priority tasks listed with C-priority tasks?

5. Do your to-do lists limit your options concerning what you should spend your time on?

6. Do you include context for each to-do item so you'll know whether it's a high-value or low-value task, and the time commitment involved?

7. Do you define your tasks narrowly and with specificity so you can quickly identify when they've been completed?

8. Do you associate each task with a specific goal?

It's time to tally your points. Remember, give yourself a score of one to five for each question based on how well you handle the issue posed by it. Once you've tallied your points, you'll know your level of proficiency.

If you scored between **32 and 40 points**, consider yourself a to-do list ninja. You're adept, a bona fide master at task management. You regularly get through your daily lists and advance your most important work along the way. It's still a good idea to read this action guide as a form of recurrent training.

If you scored between **19 and 31**, you're doing reasonably well, but could stand to improve select areas of your task management strategy. You might be feeling overwhelmed by your responsibilities at work and at home. You may also be experiencing persistent stress as your list of tasks grows by the day. Learning how to create effective to-do lists can deliver dramatic results in your productivity and time management efforts.

If you scored **18 or fewer points**, you need to rethink your approach to how you create your to-do lists. You're stressed and feel that each day spirals out of your control. You rarely, if ever, get through your to-do lists, which causes you to feel frustrated, guilty, and even incompetent. Don't beat yourself up. The good news is that you're in the right place. By the time you finish reading this action guide, you'll know how to create task lists that help you to get the important stuff done.

In the next section, we're going to explore how your emotions can hamper your productivity, even if you're working with an effective to-do list.

How Negative Emotions Impair Your Productivity

It's important to recognize the impact our emotions have on our productivity. When we're unhappy, stressed, or fearful, our productivity suffers. We feel disengaged from our work, regardless of its role in achieving our goals. We're also less creative and have more difficulty making decisions. Moreover, we lose focus and become more easily distracted.

Consequently, we get less done.

All of us go through periods during which we experience negative emotions. It's human nature. It's important to realize that such periods are temporary. We eventually regain a positive outlook that allows us to snap out of our funk and get things done.

Unfortunately, many people experience prolonged bouts of negativity. They allow their anxieties, frustrations, and insecurities take hold of their thoughts, which has a predictably dreadful impact on their productivity.

Studies show that chronic stress and fear can literally change how the brain functions. Our ability to process thoughts and make rational decisions suffers as stress hormones, such as cortisol, accumulate. Neuroscientists have discovered that, over time, this state can damage the brain, hampering our decision-making ability.

Consider that in the context of working from properly created to-do lists. Even if your lists are short, include deadlines, provide context, present minimal variability, and tasks are associated with specific goals, your results may be less than stellar. Negative emotions like fear, anger, and guilt can make it nearly impossible to concentrate and get things done.

So if you're having trouble staying productive during the workday, take stock of your emotional state. Are you struggling with feelings that are siphoning your motivation? Are you dealing with emotions that are having a toxic effect on your willpower? Is persistent negativity eroding your focus and causing you to be more easily distracted?

If so, pinpoint the reasons you're experiencing these feelings. For example, do you feel guilty and depressed because you've missed important deadlines at your job? Do you feel stressed and angry because you're being overwhelmed by too many conflicting responsibilities at home?

Once you've identified whatever is triggering your negativity, you can take steps to change your circumstances and relieve the pressure.

This may seem unrelated to your to-do lists. On the contrary, your emotional state plays a significant role in how successfully you work from your lists. Remember, your to-do list is there to help you organize tasks according to their importance and priority, and identify where to best spend your limited time. You won't be able to do that effectively if you're struggling with persistent negativity.

With this topic out of the way, let's turn our attention to the most popular to-do list strategies used today.

10 Most Popular
To-Do List Systems

There's more than one way to create an effective to-do list. This section will describe the top 10 strategies used today. You may already be familiar with some of them. Others may be new to you.

The purpose of this section isn't to highlight the best system. Rather, it's to give you a bird's-eye view of several systems so you can identify specific features that resonate with you.

This section will come in handy when we design a to-do list system that supports your workflow process. You'll be able to integrate your favorite features from other systems to build one that's perfectly-suited to you.

#1 - The Massive, All-Inclusive List

There's nothing elegant about this strategy. It is essentially a brain dump. You write down every task you can think of onto a single list.

You can already see the problems inherent in this approach. First, your list will grow too long. If you're dumping new tasks onto it each day, there's little chance you'll ever get through it.

Second, you'll have too many options. This will impair your decision-making ability. Presented with a long list of choices, you're more likely to become paralyzed with indecision than you are to take action.

Third, your list will have too much variability. Three-minute tasks will be listed next to three-hour tasks. Low-priority tasks will be listed next to high-priority tasks. You'll end up spending time on items that don't warrant your immediate attention.

There are other problems with the "massive, all-inclusive" list approach to task management. But at this point, you get the idea. This strategy leaves a lot to be desired.

It's worth pointing out that doing a brain dump is an important step toward creating an effective to-do list. But it's a *first* step. After you've written down all of the tasks you can think of, you need to organize them according to their importance, priority, context, and other elements.

We'll discuss this facet of to-do list management in more detail later. For now, it's enough to know that doing a brain dump and working from a single, comprehensive list is a terrible idea. You might *feel* productive as you complete tasks and cross them off your list. But in reality, you'll be inclined to choose easy, low-priority tasks that require minimal time to complete and leave the high-value items unaddressed.

This approach is popular. But its popularity isn't due to its effectiveness. Far from it. It's due to the lack of training most people receive regarding how to properly design a solid task management system.

I wanted to address this strategy first in order to underscore its flaws. The other nine to-do list systems also have flaws. But they're less detrimental to your long-term success.

#2 - The "Task + Starting Date + Due Date" List

The appeal of this format is its simplicity. It also introduces one of the most important elements of a proper task management system: deadlines.

As we discussed earlier, most to-do lists lack concrete deadlines. An individual may have a vague sense regarding the latest date by which a particular task must be completed, but he or she neglects to assign a formal due date to it.

This is a grave mistake. Deadlines are important because they prompt us to take action. They also help us to allocate our limited time among competing projects and tasks. Assuming our deadlines are realistic and take into account the comparative priorities of our to-do items, they increase our productivity. We not only get more things done, but we get more of the *right* things done.

This approach to creating to-do lists also introduces a second crucial feature: starting dates. Rather than leaving you with a long list of tasks and their respective due dates, it also provides the dates on which you should begin working on the tasks.

This feature is more useful than it might seem. It delivers two important benefits. First, it allows you to focus on a smaller number of to-do items. You can devote your attention to tasks that are in progress or need to be started that day. You can ignore those that have starting dates in the future.

Second, you'll be less likely to work on tasks at the last possible minute. The tasks' starting dates will prompt you to work on them early enough to meet their respective deadlines.

In contrast, consider how most people work through their to-do lists. They select items without knowing which ones can wait and which need immediate attention. Without starting dates and deadlines to inform their decisions, they address to-do items in a haphazardly fashion.

This can obliterate your productivity. You're almost guaranteed to end up working on the wrong tasks at the wrong time.

This to-do list system is imperfect in many ways. In fact, it has major flaws. But it's better than the massive, all-inclusive list described in the previous section.

#3 - The To-Do List Twosome: Master Task List + Daily Task List

This approach is the one-two punch of to-do list creation. It involves keeping two distinct lists: your master list and your daily list. As with the two previous systems we profiled, it leaves a lot to be desired. However, the fact that it makes a distinction between your "brain dump" list and your daily list makes it worthy of mention.

Here's a summary of how this system works:

Your master list is a rolling repository of every task you think of. It's where you record every item, regardless of its priority, deadline, the time required to complete it, and the project with which it's associated.

Do you intend to call a roofing contractor to get an estimate on a new roof for your home? Write it down on your master list. Need to have your truck's transmission replaced? This is where you record the task. Do you plan to research the hot biotech stock your investment advisor mentioned to you? Write it down.

You'll never get through your master list. In fact, it will probably grow with time. That's fine, according to folks who use this system. The purpose of this list is to capture the myriad tasks swimming around in your head, saving you the effort of having to remember them.

What about the *daily* list? As its name implies, this is the list you work from throughout the day. It's the one you keep near your side and review periodically to gauge your progress. Its scope is limited to the tasks you intend to complete by the end of the day.

Here's how the two lists work together:

Each evening, you would review your master list. You'd look for tasks due in the near future or those that need to be addressed in order to move other tasks forward. Once you identify these to-do items, you'd choose several and transfer them to the following day's daily list, assuming your schedule allows adequate time to address them.

Alternatively, you might review your master list every few days rather than nightly. This would entail planning your daily to-do lists a few days in advance.

This approach to task management can be effective. The key is that each task is assigned a deadline, along with notes detailing its priority, context, and the time required to complete it.

Unfortunately, few people using this to-do list system go to those lengths. They cut corners and end up dealing with the same problems seen with other systems: lists that grow to the point of becoming overwhelming; to-do items that must be carried forward day after day; and valuable time wasted on low-priority tasks.

#4 - The "3+2" Strategy

This to-do list system follows a simple formula: three big tasks and two small tasks.

Each day, you select the five items you'll work on. (Or better yet, select them the night before.) The big items should take between one and two hours to complete. The small items should take 30 minutes or less.

You've probably already noticed one of the main strengths of the "3+2" strategy. It limits the number of tasks on your daily to-do list. There are five. No more. No less.

Another strength is that it defines the scope of each task with respect to the time allotted to complete it. The big ones can be finished in under two hours while the small ones should take less than 30 minutes. (Tasks that take longer than two hours to complete can usually be broken down into smaller tasks.)

This feature of the "3+2" strategy makes it compatible with popular time management strategies like the Pomodoro Technique and timeboxing.

For example, schedule four pomodoros - each composed of a 25-minute work segment and 5-minute break - to complete one of your big tasks. Allocate time boxes that give you the time you need to complete your smaller tasks.

The "3+2" strategy improves your focus by limiting the scope of your task list. With only five items to work on, you're less susceptible to distractions. You'll also less likely to suffer paralysis by analysis, a state in which you're unable to make decisions because you're overanalyzing a situation.

This approach also minimizes task switching. Because your to-do list will carry fewer tasks to focus on, you'll be less inclined to switch back and forth between them. Instead, you'll focus on one task until you've completed it or you're unable to take it further. This reduces switching costs, the loss in productivity that results from jumping between unrelated tasks.

The "3+2" strategy isn't without inherent flaws. For example, no mention is made of assigning context to each to-do item. It may seem as if context isn't important given that your to-do list carries so few options. But context is still useful to ensure your most important work gets done as early as possible.

Also, no mention is made regarding the origin of each day's five tasks. From where do they spring? How are they identified? Are they selected from a master task list or do you brainstorm them at the beginning of each day?

These questions have no concrete answers.

Another downside of this system is its lack of flexibility. It's rigid. It doesn't adapt.

For example, suppose that tomorrow is a perfect day to complete a long list of small tasks. Each item will only take a few minutes to address. You need to pay bills, mail your Netflix DVDs, schedule a dentist appointment, email a friend, clean the toilet in your master bathroom, etc. The "3+2" strategy doesn't allow for this type of day. You can only pick two small tasks to work on.

Personally, if I were to use the "3+2" strategy, here's how I would do it: I'd maintain a master list of every to-do item that comes to mind. I'd make certain each item was specific in scope and attached to a goal. I'd assign deadlines and add contextual details. Each evening, I'd pick my three large tasks and two small tasks for the following day.

It's nowhere near perfect. But that's how I'd approach it.

#5 - The 1-3-5 Rule

The "1-3-5 rule" is an extrapolation of the "3+2 strategy" described in the previous section. Here, you choose one big task, three medium-sized tasks, and five small tasks to complete during the day.

While the "3+2 strategy" limits your focus to five tasks, the "1-3-5 rule" expands the number to nine.

The first advantage to this approach is that it gives you more flexibility than the "3+2 strategy." Not only does it allow you to choose more items to get done each day (nine vs. five), but it also presents three categories rather than just two. The inclusion of "medium-sized" tasks is useful because it helps you to better manage your calendar.

For example, suppose you have a task you know will require 45 minutes to complete. With the "3+2 strategy," it falls outside the definition of a big task (one that takes between one and two hours).

It also falls outside the definition of a small task (one that takes 30 minutes or less). The "1-3-5 rule" offers a place for such items.

Another advantage of this system is that it encourages you to focus on high-value tasks. In that, it has a lot in common with the "3+2 strategy." Because you're limited in the number of items you can include on your list, you'll be more inclined to include those that have a high priority.

A third advantage is that you won't fall prey to overoptimism. It's common to think we can accomplish more than is actually possible during any given day. So we pack our to-do lists with a large number of tasks, many of which invariably never get done. By limiting the number of tasks to nine, the "1-3-5 rule" solves that problem.

As you've probably guessed, the "1-3-5 rule" suffers from the same imperfections as the "3+2 strategy." First, no mention is made of giving context to the to-do items. Second, no mention is made of a master list from which the nine daily tasks are chosen. And third, this approach doesn't allow for the use of a batch task list.

We'll talk more batch task lists in an upcoming section. For now, it's enough to know that they're an important part of a sound task management strategy.

The "1-3-5 rule" can be an effective to-do list system with a few modifications. But there is an even better approach, which I'll show you later in this action guide.

For now, remember the basics of this strategy. You may want to incorporate a few of its features into your system.

#6 - The Project-Based System

This system entails categorizing your to-do items based on the projects with which they're associated. In the end, you're left with multiple lists, one per project.

For example, suppose you want to remodel your kitchen. You'd create a list for this particular project with the following tasks:

- Plan the layout of your new kitchen
- Pick the types of cabinets you want
- Select your preferred countertop material
- Choose light fixtures
- Explore your backsplash options
- List the appliances you want to replace
- Look for a new refrigerator to match the design of your new kitchen
- Call three contractors to solicit bids

You'd create a separate list for a different project you'd like to complete, such as buying a new car. This list might have the following tasks:

- Determine how much money you can spend
- Compile a list of makes and models you like
- Narrow down the list to three options
- Visit the car dealership
- Test drive the cars
- Negotiate the price
- Find the best form of financing
- Get approved for a loan
- Sign the paperwork to take ownership

Task-level context is inherent in this system as your lists are organized according to project. Any item on a particular list is there because it's directly related to the project for which the list was created.

Another advantage of this system is that it gives you a bird's-eye view of your multiple projects in progress. You can select tasks to work on depending on which project you want to move forward.

One of the drawbacks to a project-based system is that it offers very little structure with regard to how you spend your day. Rather than working from a single to-do list that has been created to maximize your productivity, you pick and choose tasks from multiple lists. This feature creates too much variability. There are too many options, which opens the door to task switching and its attendant costs.

Another flaw is the limited context given to each task. I mentioned above that task-level context was inherent in this system. But it is defined solely by project. Tasks are not given context related to the time required to complete them, their respective priorities, or the energy needed to work on them.

You probably also noticed the absence of a batch task list. (Again, we'll talk about batch lists in an upcoming section.)

As with the other to-do list strategies we've covered thus far, this system can be effective. But it suffers from major weaknesses.

We can do better.

#7 - The 3-MIT Approach

This strategy may be familiar to you. It was popularized by Leo Babauta of ZenHabits.net, although he openly admits it originated elsewhere.

MIT is an acronym. It stands for "most important task." It's the highest-priority item on your to-do list. It's the one thing you must complete during the course of a given day.

The original strategy called for identifying a single MIT, and focusing on its completion to the exclusion of everything else. Only after completing this item would you turn your attention to other items.

The "3-MIT" approach is a common variant. In fact, it's probably more common than the single-MIT approach because it's more practical for a greater number of people.

As its name implies, you select three high-priority tasks to focus on during your day. Whatever else happens, you must get these three items done.

Depending on how much time you need to complete your three MITs, there will be days when you get through your to-do list early. You'll have plenty of time remaining to work on other to-do tasks. There may also be days during which you have to work late in order to complete your three MITs.

As with any task management system, the effectiveness of the "3-MIT" approach is in its execution. The details are left to the user to define.

For example, how do you choose your three MITs? Do you link them to specific goals and give them context accordingly? Do you estimate in advance how much time each one will take to complete so you can avoid overextending yourself given your schedule and availability? How do you integrate your MITs with your calendar to ensure they receive the time and attention they need? How do you make certain small, but important tasks get done in a timely fashion?

You can see that this system is open-ended. It defines a few guidelines, but offers considerable flexibility in terms of their application. Unfortunately, this latitude can be a liability if you're currently struggling with your to-do lists. It poses too much freedom.

If you struggle with procrastination, are regularly waylaid by distractions, and suffer a lack of motivation, an open-ended task management strategy isn't a good solution. A structured system with well-defined rules and less latitude is likely to be more useful.

Having said that, the idea of focusing on just a few MITs each day is a practical one. It's a feature you may decide to incorporate as part of the strategy you design for yourself. So it's worth keeping in mind as we explore how to create the perfect to-do list.

Let's quickly cover the final three task management systems commonly used today. Up next: the Kanban method.

#8 - The Kanban Method

The Kanban method is a more visual approach to task management than the systems we've covered thus far. It's a great to-do list strategy if you enjoy seeing your projects and tasks in various stages of completion.

Here's how it works:

Grab a cork board and a stack of Post-It notes. Make three columns on your board. Title the left column "To Do." Title the middle column "Doing." Title the right column "Done."

You can probably see where this is going.

The Kanban method involves writing down each new task on a Post-It note, one task per note, and sticking it in the "To Do" column. There it remains until you're ready to address it. When you start working on a task, you move its associated Post-It note to the "Doing" column. When you've completed the task, you move its Post-It note to the "Done" column.

This strategy of managing to-do items has a few notable advantages over other strategies. First, it provides a visual representation of your projects and tasks. This makes it easy to identify high-value items that need your immediate attention. It also makes it easy to prioritize items according to their respective due dates.

Second, the Kanban method allows you to track the progress of individual tasks. You can tell at a glance whether a task is yet to be started, is currently under way, or has been completed.

A third advantage of the Kanban system is that tasks can be easily associated with larger projects. This provides valuable task-level context. You can arrange the Post-It notes so that it's easy to see how individual tasks flow within a larger construct.

Fourth, you can use different colored Post-It notes to represent varying levels of priority. For example, use red for high-priority items, yellow for medium-priority items, and blue for low-priority items. The Kanban method's biggest strength is its visual presentation.

You don't have to use a cork board. You can use a dry erase board to the same effect. Keep in mind, this will limit your ability to rearrange tasks based on their changing priorities and your availability.

In the last few years, a number of options have surfaced that make it possible to use the Kanban method online. You no longer need to hang a cork board on your wall or set up a dry erase board. You can use apps like Trello, KanbanFlow, LeanKit, and Kanbanote.

Each app poses its own set of strengths and weaknesses. If you're interested in playing with the Kanban method online, I recommend Trello. It's free and user-friendly.

One of the downsides to using the Kanban method is that it's easy to lose track of small tasks. For instance, suppose your master to-do list contains more than 100 items that have yet to be worked on. Those items would encompass a lot of Post-It notes organized in a single, linear format (presumably, in the "To Do" column). There's a fair chance your eyes will gloss over some of them, and you'll miss a few considered to be high-value.

Color-coding can be an effective solution; different colors can be used to indicate task-level priority. But even then, your ability to monitor a large volume of to-do items will be limited.

There's a lot to like about the Kanban method. But it's imperfect. Note its basic features and think about how you might incorporate some of them into your personal to-do list system.

#9 - The Matrix System

The Matrix system was popularized by the late Stephen Covey, author of the acclaimed book *The Seven Habits of Highly Effective People*. It is also known as the "Eisenhower Box." The same principles apply to both. It's a tool used to decide how to allocate one's time among competing tasks.

A matrix is made up of four quadrants titled as follows:

1. Important - Urgent
2. Important - Not Urgent
3. Not Important - Urgent
4. Not Important - Not Urgent

Tasks are assigned to the quadrants according to their respective priorities. Those placed in the first quadrant should be addressed immediately. Those in the second quadrant are less dire, but should be scheduled to ensure they're addressed at some point in the near future. Tasks in the third quadrant can be delegated to others while tasks in the fourth quadrant can be abandoned.

This system provides an easy way to see which to-do items warrant your attention and which can be ignored. You'll be able to easily identify items associated with your most important work. They'll be found in Quadrants I and II. You'll also be able to disregard those that will have minimal impact. These will be found in Quadrant IV.

For example, a project with an impending deadline (e.g. 4:00 p.m. today) should be placed in Quadrant I. It needs your immediate attention.

Your weekly review can be placed in Quadrant II. It's important, but can wait until later. Schedule it so that it doesn't fall through the cracks.

Select meetings might be well-suited for Quadrant III. They're urgent in the sense that they occur at scheduled times. But some are likely to have minor value to you. Try to have someone attend the meetings in your place.

Returning unsolicited calls from salespeople should be relegated to Quadrant IV. The activity is unimportant and non-urgent. You won't suffer a major consequence if it is never addressed.

The upside of the Matrix system is that it encourages you to focus on tasks that are consistent with your goals. You'll find yourself constantly asking "*Is this task necessary?*" as you review your matrix. Unnecessary tasks can be discarded without guilt. You'll end up spending more time on high-value items and wasting less time on low-value ones.

One of the drawbacks of this approach is that it doesn't require you to provide context for the tasks in the matrix's four quadrants. No mention is made concerning how long each task will take to complete, nor its connection with other tasks and projects.

Another problem is that the matrix may grow to the point that it presents too many options. That is, you may find a large number of tasks in Quadrant II, and have difficulty choosing which ones to work on given your limited availability.

As with the Kanban method, there's a lot to like about the Matrix system (or Eisenhower Box) despite its flaws. You may find that some of its features are well suited to the way you work.

In a few moments, we're going to create a personal to-do list system that will help you to get the important stuff done. First, let's take a look at the final - and arguably the most popular - task management system used today: Getting Things Done (GTD).

#10 - Getting Things Done (GTD)

David Allen's Getting Things Done is one of the most celebrated task management systems in use today. Interestingly, it has as many detractors as it has advocates (for reasons we'll get to in a moment).

Here are the basics:

You have a lot of stuff swimming around in your head. Most of it remains uncategorized in terms of context, priority, and intended outcomes.

For example, you may be thinking of your brother's birthday, the shortage of paper towels in your kitchen, and your daughter's upcoming piano recital. You might be spending mental energy on the fact that you need to put gas in your car, mow the lawn, and buy bug spray to deal with the ants in your bathroom.

Meanwhile, your tooth hurts, suggesting it's time to see the dentist. Your back hurts, indicating a doctors visit might be in order. And a little voice in your head whispers that you should make exercise a bigger priority.

These items float around in your mind. There's no plan to take action on them, which leaves open loops. We want to get these things done, but we haven't committed ourselves to their completion. Open loops cause us stress.

GTD seeks to get this stuff out of your head and onto a list. It makes each item actionable, thereby closing the open loops. Once items are on a master list, you spend time organizing them according to context. Part of this process entails creating multiple lists and placing items where they belong. A weekly review is performed to stay on top of things.

That's a simplified explanation of GTD (entire books have been written about it). It will suffice for our purposes.

This strategy offers several important features. First, it forces you to add context to each task. This is inherent in the process of "dumping" everything onto a master list and then moving tasks to other, more refined lists.

Second, it separates tasks based on importance. Part of GTD involves creating a "next actions" list and a "someday/maybe" list. Both are useful. The former encourages you to keep your important work moving forward. The latter allows you to capture ideas that may have value, but need further consideration before that value can be determined.

Third, GTD advises performing a weekly review. This review is not an afterthought. Allen refers to it as one of the keys to being successful using GTD.

Fourth, it's as flexible as you need it to be. While GTD provides structure, it doesn't force you to adhere to specific tactics. It offers a framework that gives you enough flexibility to create your own personalized approach.

Having said the above, there are a few challenges with using GTD. First, it focuses more on processing the ideas in your head than actually getting them done.

Second, not enough attention is given to how each item captured on the "brain dump" list relates to your goals. While you're forced to give the items context and place them on more refined lists, you're not required to link them to specific objectives.

Third, the flexibility inherent in GTD can prove to be

detrimental to some users. Oftentimes, people who struggle with task management need *more* constraints on their freedom, not less. Such constraints can help them to rein in bad habits and improve their focus.

Fourth, it's easy to get overwhelmed while using GTD. This system is effective for getting stuff out of your head and onto paper (or into an online note-taking app). But not everything in your head deserves a place on your to-do lists. Much of it will be irrelevant to your goals. Much of it will waste your time. Recording every item can make you feel as if you're getting buried under a mountain of minutiae.

Getting Things Done is popular as a strategy for organizing tasks and creating to-do lists. There's no doubt about that. But the more you research it, the more you'll find that many people have tried and abandoned it.

It's worth asking *"Is GTD actually effective?"* We'll take a closer look at this question in the next section.

Getting Things Done: Is It Effective?

Getting Things Done is a system that seems highly effective when you first adopt it. You spend a lot of time getting stuff out of your head and organizing it according to context. These are crucial steps toward identifying your most important work. The fact that they reduce your stress - trying to remember everything is stressful! - is another signal of the system's effectiveness.

As time passes, however, you may become disenchanted with GTD. It's a common experience. The system's rigorous focus on "next actions" detracts from project-level focus. You begin to feel like a short-order cook, pumping out "next actions" without stopping to consider the bigger picture.

Another problem is that using GTD doesn't provide a method for choosing among competing tasks. There's no workflow management system in place to ensure the important work gets done and the less important work remains on the back burner.

GTD is also weak with regard to attaching tasks to specific goals. The link to goals is severed at the outset due to the system's hard focus on "next actions" rather than projects. Without an emphasis on projects, GTD lacks a meaningful framework for goal setting and goal achievement.

Some people claim that setting goals is not only unnecessary and useless, but harmful in the long run when it comes to task management. I disagree. Goals provide vision, focus, and motivation. They also give us a gauge by which to measure our progress.

In my opinion, one of the biggest downfalls of GTD is that it doesn't distinguish between high-value and low-value tasks. The priority is to get things done while little attention is given to whether the *right* things are getting done.

Have people used GTD to effectively create to-do lists and successfully manage their task workflow? Yes. But just as many have found that GTD is insufficient in many ways, including some of the ways I described above.

GTD isn't without practical, beneficial features. I encourage you to look for those that might prove useful in your own strategy.

In the next section, I'll show you how to create to-do lists that work. Roll up your sleeves because we're going to build them from scratch.

How To Create
The Perfect To-Do List

This is where the rubber meets the road. We're going to take everything we've covered thus far and use it to build an effective to-do list system.

The system we're about to create will make it easier for you to get your most important work done on time. It will reduce your stress, eliminate your frustration, and help you to focus and avoid distractions along the way.

Most people underestimate the importance of their to-do lists. They misjudge the impact their lists have on their productivity. As you read the following sections, I encourage you to take the opposite view. Recognize that your to-do list plays a vital role in how your day progresses. An effective system will not only help you to stay on top of your workflow, but will also help you manage your daily life.

Let's build the perfect to-do list.

Step 1: Isolate Current Tasks From Future Tasks

In the section *10 Most Popular To-Do List Systems*, I noted that one of the strengths of David Allen's GTD system is its use of multiple lists. It advocates the use of a "next actions" list and a "someday/maybe" list.

We can refine this practice to squeeze more value from it.

First, use a "current task" list to decide how to allocate your time and attention each day. This list will carry the to-do items that must be completed before the day ends.

Second, use a "future task" list to keep track of all the items that will need your attention at some point. You won't use this list during the course of your workday. Instead, you'll refer to it at the end of the day to create the following day's to-do list.

This simple step, separating current tasks from future tasks, is critical. It can mean the difference between getting high-value work done on time and becoming overwhelmed under a mountain of tasks with varying priorities and deadlines.

Many people work from a single, massive to-do list that grows by the day as new items are added to it. This practice can be discouraging because there's no end in sight. Those who work in this manner never manage to get through their lists, so they always feel as if they're merely treading water.

Separating current and future tasks short-circuits this feeling. The massive list, the one that contains all future tasks, is set aside. No attention is paid to it during the workday. In its stead, the current task list takes the spotlight. Its limited scope - remember, it only carries items that are to be completed that day - reduces stress and removes the sense of overwhelm.

This is a slight deviation from the "next actions" list used in GTD. That list doesn't limit your focus to the current day. As GTD's creator David Allen noted, it is intended to list the *next physical, visible activity that needs to be engaged in, in order to move the current reality toward completion.* As such, the "next actions" list could potentially go on for several pages.

This is a crucial distinction. You'll find that completing each day's to-do list will motivate and inspire you. There's something invigorating about crossing off every item from your list. You'll feel as if the day is a productive success.

Imagine experiencing that positive feeling day after day.

Step 2: Define Tasks By Desired Outcomes

The only reason to do something is if doing it moves you closer toward achieving a specific goal. For example, few people study calculus in their free time. Most do so in order to complete schoolwork, prepare for a test, or broaden their skill set.

Likewise, few people clean out their rain gutters for enjoyment. They do so to prevent water damage to their roofs.

We take action to effect specific outcomes. Otherwise, why would we spend time and effort doing things that prevent us from pursuing activities we find more enjoyable (for example, binge-watching our favorite TV series on Netflix)?

Consider that notion in the context of your to-do lists. How often have you failed to complete tasks - or even start working on them - because they appeared to have little importance to you? Chances are, the tasks weren't attached to specific goals you wanted to achieve.

The simplest way to get through your daily to-do list is to assign a "why" to each item found on it. Know the reason the item is on your list. Determine why you need to get it done. Write the reason down next to the task.

For example, suppose your to-do list carries the item "call my parents." You probably have a reason to call them, if only to check in and see how they're doing. Alternatively, you might want to invite them to breakfast or ask them about a family-related matter.

The point is, calling your parents is intended to accomplish a specific goal. Write down that goal, or desired outcome, next to the task. You'll be more likely to follow through on it if you see the reason for doing it.

It's not enough to keep the reasons for doing tasks in your head. You must write them down. Doing so makes it material. A reason written down is more real than a reason bouncing around in your head.

You'll find that when you associate tasks with specific outcomes, you'll feel more compelled to get them done. Taking action will signify progress toward goals you hope to achieve - goals that are important to you.

This is one of the defining traits of an effective to-do list.

Step 3: Break Projects Down To Individual Tasks

You've probably heard this joke: *How do you eat an elephant? One bite at a time.*

It illustrates an important concept related to task management. The only way to complete any project is to first break it down to its constituent parts. A project is moved forward by working on the individual tasks that are incumbent to its completion.

You know this intuitively. But do you apply the principle to your daily to-do lists?

When we're faced with a large project, it's difficult to know where to begin. Consequently, we become more prone to distractions. Any distraction is preferable to grappling with an endeavor for which we lack direction and momentum.

This is the reason many to-do "items" remain unfinished at the end of the day. They're technically projects. They're too large in scope and can seem overwhelming, which causes us to procrastinate. We ultimately carry them forward to the following day, where they continue to nag us.

If we don't invest the time to break down projects to their smaller, more manageable pieces, this motivation-crushing process is likely to repeat itself day after day.

Let's look at an example.

Suppose one of the items on your master list is "clean the house." This is a project, one that can potentially take hours to complete. Listed as a single item, it's overwhelming. It's difficult to know where to start.

So let's break down the project to smaller tasks, each of which offers focus and can be completed in less time. Here's a starter list:

- Wash the dishes
- Clean the kitchen countertops
- Mop the kitchen floor
- Clean the downstairs bathroom
- Clean the upstairs bathrooms
- Vacuum the floors
- Dust the furniture

Notice that each of the above tasks is actionable. And importantly, each one is independent of the others. You don't have to address them in any particular order.

This gives you flexibility in how you schedule time to complete the tasks. Rather than setting aside four hours to "clean the house," you can set aside 10 minutes to wash the dishes, 15 minutes to mop the kitchen floor, and 30 minutes to clean the downstairs bathroom.

Breaking projects down into smaller tasks makes them seem more doable. It also allows you to focus your limited time and attention on tasks according to their priority and value. For example, washing the dishes may be a high-priority item that warrants your immediate attention. Meanwhile, vacuuming the floors can be postponed until tomorrow without consequence.

It's important to make the distinction.

Make sure your to-do lists are limited to actionable tasks, not projects. If an item requires more than one action, it is a project that can - and should - be broken down. By breaking them down, you'll enjoy better focus and get important work done more quickly.

Step 4: Assign A Deadline To Each Task

You already know the importance of deadlines. They help us to focus our time and attention on important tasks. They help us to organize our calendars. They encourage us to take action. Studies also show they improve our performance.

Ultimately, deadlines increase our efficiency and productivity, spurring us to get important stuff done.

For this reason, every task on your master to-do list should have a deadline associated with it. The date doesn't have to be written in stone. It can change as the priority and urgency of the task to which it's attached changes.

Nor must the date be precise. Your task list may include to-do items that need to be addressed at some point, but can be put on the back burner for now. A due date of "mid-August," rather than "August 14," may suffice if the task isn't due for several months.

Attaching a deadline to every item on your master to-do list makes it easier to know which tasks to select for your daily to-do list. You can tell at a glance which items need your attention tomorrow and which ones can be shelved until a future date.

Having said that, it's not enough to assign a deadline to each item. The manner in which you do so is equally important. It will influence your morale, motivation, and ability to focus. Your strategy in setting deadlines will dictate whether they are effective.

Here are a few tips…

First, make sure each deadline is realistic. It does no good to assign an impossible due date to a task. Doing so will only cause you stress, frustration, and discouragement.

Second, come up with a reason for each due date. For example, suppose it's summertime and your child is due for a dental checkup. You'd probably want to schedule a dentist appointment by August 31 to ensure it gets done before your child returns to school. You have a reason to act. The reason makes the deadline genuine.

When a deadline is set without a reason - that is, the date is arbitrarily chosen - there's less impetus to take action. The sense of urgency is artificial.

Third, give yourself less time than you think you need. I mentioned Parkinson's Law in the section *Why You're Not Finishing Your List Of To-Do Items*. That law states "work expands so as to fill the time available for its completion." We tend to allow ourselves too much time to get things done. You'll find that narrowing the window will improve your focus and result in greater efficiency and productivity.

There's no reason to dread deadlines. On the contrary, you should look forward to applying them to every item on your master task list. They'll help you to avoid distractions and give you the motivation, inspiration, and energy you need to move your most important work forward.

Step 5: Limit The Number Of Current Tasks To Seven

One of the most common problems with to-do lists is that they're too long. Those that start with just a few tasks invariably grow to include dozens. It's no wonder so many people are unable to get through their to-do lists. Doing so is practically impossible!

On the one hand, this circumstance is understandable. During the course of any given day, new projects are conceived and new tasks are born from them.

But that doesn't mean you should add them to your daily task list. In fact, doing so would be setting yourself up for failure.

I strongly recommend limiting the number of items on your daily to-do list to seven. This is a manageable number. Assuming no single task requires hours to complete, it's possible to get through your entire list by the end of the day.

We talked about the "3+2" strategy and the "1-3-5 rule" in the section *10 Most Popular To-Do List Systems*. Both methods limit the number of tasks that appear on your daily lists. Both get this aspect of task management right. They keep your list short so you can get through it each day. As a result, you'll avoid the sense of overwhelm and self-guilt that accompanies failure in that department.

Allow me to clarify something. I mentioned limiting your daily to-do list to seven items. You might be wondering how, at that rate, you'll get through the hundreds of tasks on your master to-do list, which grows longer each day.

My "limit-to-seven" suggestion refers solely to tasks that require at least 15 minutes to complete. You'll find that many of the tasks on your master list can be handled within one or two minutes. Following are a few examples:

- Make your bed
- Check your voicemail
- Sort your mail
- Start a load of laundry
- Make a dinner reservation
- Subscribe to a newsletter (like mine!)

- Return a phone call
- Add a plug-in to your Wordpress blog
- Declutter your desktop
- Decide what to have for dinner

These are "tiny tasks" that don't belong on your daily to-do list. Why? Because they could potentially cause the list to grow to dozens of items.

Instead, I recommend keeping a "batch list." We'll talk about this practice in more detail in the upcoming section *How To Maintain A Well-Oiled To-Do List System*. For now, recognize that tiny tasks like "sort your mail" should not be among the seven items on your daily to-do list.

Step 6: Organize Tasks By Project, Type, Or Location

It's common to treat the master task list as a rolling "brain dump." New tasks are added to the bottom of the list as you think of them. The problem is, if you leave it in that condition, it will eventually become overwhelming.

Even if you give each item a deadline and provide various types of context, your list will become burdensome over time. You'll find it increasingly difficult to manage tasks. A lot of items will end up falling through the cracks.

Imagine reviewing 20 pages of to-do items. My own master list used to be much longer before I learned how to create effective lists. Finding specific tasks and managing the associated projects took too much time.

No longer. I now organize tasks based on various contexts: by project, type, and location. I maintain multiple lists accordingly. (Note that these lists are separate and distinct from my daily to-do list.)

Task-level context is an important part of any to-do list system. It defines how long items should take to complete. It reminds you of the reasons to get them done. It encourages you to focus on tasks that have the highest priorities given your goals.

For these reasons, categorize each task on your master to-do list using the following three contexts:

1. Project
2. Type
3. Location

I recommend creating a separate list for each project, each type of task, and each location. For example, the following projects would warrant their own lists:

- Write a book
- Remodel my kitchen
- Buy a car

The following types of tasks would also warrant their own lists:

- Analytical work
- Creative work
- Mindless work

Likewise, the following locations would warrant their own lists:

- At the office
- At home
- On the road

Categorizing to-do items by project, type, and location will keep you organized. It will also help you to choose tasks for your daily list that complement your circumstances.

For example, "vacuum the living room" is clearly a location-based task. You must be at home to do it. If you plan to be at the office all day, you wouldn't add this item to your daily list.

Some tasks can - and should - be assigned to more than one context.

For example, consider the project "Write a Book." One of your early tasks is to "write the first draft of chapter 1." This task is already categorized by project. But if the only time you're able to write is while you're at home, it should also be categorized by location. Moreover, keep in mind that writing is creative work that requires mental energy. As such, it may be useful to categorize it by type of activity. That way, you can schedule it on your calendar for times when your energy levels are high.

If you're creating to-do lists on paper, assigning multiple contexts to tasks can be problematic. One solution is to color code them.

For example, the task "write the first draft of chapter 1" is already found under the project "write a book." Color-coding for that context is unnecessary. But you can use colored pens to assign location and activity type contexts. Red can signify "at home" and blue can signify "creative work."

This is an imperfect solution, of course. A better approach is to use an online tool, such as Todoist. It offers tagging and labeling features with a palette of colors that make it easy to organize to-do items by multiple contexts.

One last note before we move on. You may find it useful to keep a separate list for high-priority, high-value to-do items. Some people call this a HIT list, or high-impact task list.

Personally, I find the use of a HIT list to be overkill. I already assign a priority to every item on my various lists. Creating an additional list for high-impact items is unnecessary. It hampers my efficiency rather than improves it.

But I wanted to mention the practice in the event you find it helps your workflow. Remember, this is about creating a system that works for *you*.

Step 7: Prune Your List Of Unnecessary Tasks

One of the most important things you can do is to keep your master to-do list clean. You need to prune the list on a regular basis, purging tasks that are no longer necessary or consistent with your goals. Otherwise, it can quickly become unmanageable as you add new items to it each day.

Pruning your list helps you to keep it under control. You'll be able to more easily identify important projects and their associated tasks. Task management is made simpler when irrelevant items are removed, or crossed off, your list.

Pruning also increases your efficiency. It limits your master list to tasks that advance your most important work. Consequently, you won't waste valuable time and attention on nonessential activities.

What types of tasks are candidates for removal? Look for these four items:

1. Wishes
2. Unclear tasks
3. Trivial tasks
4. Resolutions

Wishes are typically phrased as projects rather than actionable tasks. For example, you might wish to "remodel your kitchen." You may wish to "take your family to Kauai next summer." Wishes are overly broad in scope and rarely essential to achieving well-defined goals. As such, they should be removed from your master to-do list.

Keep these items on a wish list.

Unclear tasks are those that lack context. You'll sometimes find they're in that state because they don't warrant your attention. They hang in limbo until you notice them.

An example would be to "call John." Why do you need to call John? How will doing so move your important work forward? Are there consequences if you fail to make the call? If so, what are they?

If a task on your master list is unclear, reevaluate its value in light of your goals. It may be a good candidate for removal.

Trivial tasks can be eliminated without repercussions. These are random items that are recorded when they surface, and promptly forgotten. Your master list will accumulate them. That's its purpose - to clear your head of things that are difficult to remember and organize. But you'll find that, under closer examination, many of these items can - and should be - removed from the list.

Resolutions are promises. They differ from normal to-do items because they typically require a change in habit. For example, you might resolve to "exercise," "lose weight," or "learn Spanish." It's fine to have such goals, of course. But don't confuse them with actionable tasks.

Remove all resolutions from your master to-do list. They don't belong there. Instead, put them on a separate "lifestyle goals" list and treat them as projects. Then, when you're ready to act on one of them, create a separate list for it. Break it down to small, actionable tasks and assign deadlines.

A large, cumbersome master to-do list is discouraging. If you allow it to grow unchecked, it can slowly erode your motivation and crush your creativity. Keep it clean by regularly pruning unnecessary tasks. Doing so will make your list feel more *alive* because every task on it will have a specific purpose.

With periodic pruning, you'll be able to more easily identify important tasks for your daily to-do lists. You'll also spend less time on insignificant items, greatly increasing your productivity along the way.

Step 8: Estimate The Amount Of Time Each Task Will Take To Complete

You should know how long each to-do item on your master list will take you to finish. This information allows you to choose tasks for your daily list based on how much time you'll have available to work on them. If you know each task's estimated completion time, you can create realistic to-do lists. You can avoid saddling yourself with tasks that need to be carried over to the next day.

Most people neglect to take this step. Sadly, it's one of the most damaging omissions they can make. It can mean the difference between getting through their to-do lists and feeling frustrated and overwhelmed by them at the end of the day.

In order to calculate a task's estimated completion time, you must know what is required to do the task. This includes tools, information, and input from others.

For example, suppose one of the tasks on your to-do list is to "finish the accounts receivable report for boss." In order to complete the report, you may need input from your company's sales department. You might also need to refer to last week's accounts receivable and cash flow reports. How long will it take you to obtain the necessary information and resources? These requirements should be taken into account when estimating the task's completion time.

Review your master list and assign a time estimate to each item. Whether the item will take 15 minutes or 3 hours, write down the estimate next to it.

Resist the temptation to guess. We tend to be overly optimistic regarding our ability to get things done. We underestimate the time we need. Be aware of this tendency.

Come up with a *realistic* estimate based on the resources you'll need (including input from others) and the challenges you're likely to encounter along the way.

If you're familiar with the task, you'll know what resources you need and how much time it will take to complete it. You'll be able to assign a reasonably accurate estimate. If you're unfamiliar with the task, talk to someone who has worked on it in the past. Ask that person how much time it usually takes him or her.

As you assign estimated completion times to the to-do items on your master list, you'll face an interesting conundrum. I noted above that we tend to underestimate the amount of time we'll need to complete tasks. We're inclined to be overly optimistic. However, we also tend to give ourselves too much time to get things done.

For example, take mowing the lawn. Suppose a realistic completion time is 45 minutes. In our optimism, we convince ourselves that we can finish the job in under 30 minutes. Yet, because there's no urgency behind the task, we give ourselves an hour and a half.

This leniency is dangerous because it impairs our productivity. Recall Parkinson's Law: "Work expands so as to fill the time available for its completion." Although you can realistically mow your lawn in 45 minutes, you'll take an hour and a half to do it if you allow yourself that much time.

Keep Parkinson's Law in mind as you assign estimated completion times to your to-do items. It will help you to drastically reduce the amount of time you need to complete tasks. As a result, you'll get more done and enjoy more free time to pursue other interests.

Step 9: Lead Each Task With An Active Verb

Sometimes, all you need is the right word to spur you to action. Verbs have that power. Put them in front of your to-do items and you'll be more inclined to get the items done.

When you phrase a task with a verb, the task comes alive. It goes from being a mere line item on your to-do list to being an actionable assignment. The verb triggers something in the brain, prompting it to focus on completing the item.

Let's take a look at a few examples. Following are "tasks" (technically, they're little more than notes) that lack verbs:

- Laundry
- Sandra's birthday cake
- Accounts receivable report
- Car tires
- Breakfast with parents

Notice how the tasks lack emotional and motivational power. We can fix that by adding verbs to them:

- Start a load of laundry
- Buy a cake for Sandra's birthday
- Finish the accounts receivable report
- Check the pressure in my car's tires
- Call parents to plan breakfast date

Notice how the verbs (*start*, *buy*, *finish*, *check*, and *call*) tell us exactly what to do. There's no ambiguity. You don't have to guess at the type of activity the task involves. The verb defines it.

Also, notice how the verbs make it easier to estimate task completion times. It's difficult to know how long the task "laundry" will take. But you can "start a load of laundry" in five minutes.

Not just any verb will do. There's an art to choosing the right ones. The key is to be specific.

For example, consider the to-do item "contact Bob about the TPS report." The verb "contact" is helpful, but imprecise. It can mean any of the following:

- Call Bob on the phone
- Email Bob
- Send Bob a text message
- Stop by Bob's office
- Leave Bob a message in his inbox

There's value in choosing the precise verb that defines the task. Again, be specific. Will you call Bob or email him? Will you text him or stop by his office?

The right verbs encourage execution. They encourage you to take action. The wrong ones do the opposite. They encourage procrastination. Verbs like *explore*, *plan*, and *touch base* lack specificity. As a result, they're less effective than verbs like *research*, *draft*, and *call*. These latter choices have more impact because they imply specific actions. They leave nothing open to interpretation.

Phrasing tasks with the right action verbs will motivate you to take action on them. You'll be less susceptible to distractions and less likely to procrastinate because you'll know exactly what you need to do.

The result? You'll get through your daily to-do lists more quickly, getting more done in less time.

Step 10: Note Which Tasks Require Input From Others

Some of the tasks on your daily to-do list will require input from other people. For example, you might be working on a team-based project and need certain team members to complete specific tasks before you can address the ones for which you're responsible.

Even if you're working alone, others' input may be vital to your workflow. For instance, the accounts receivable report you've been tasked to complete might require input from someone in your sales department. The conference call you intend to hold may require information you've asked a coworker to obtain for you.

It's important to know, at a glance, which items on your task list require action from other people. David Allen's GTD advocates the creation of a separate "waiting for" list. This list would include every task for which you're waiting for someone to act.

Personally, I think the use of a "waiting for" list is overkill. If you've followed the previous nine steps in creating your master list, context-based lists, and daily lists, you'll do fine without it. In fact, a "waiting for" list would just overcomplicate your task management system.

Here's my recommendation: write a short note next to each to-do item for which you're waiting for someone's input. Detail the type of input you need, its format (email, phone call, report, spreadsheet, etc.), and the date you expect it to be delivered.

The expected delivery date will prompt you to follow up with the person if you don't receive his or her input in a timely fashion. To that end, it will help you to set expectations for others and hold them accountable for needed deliverables. This is critical if your workflow depends on them taking action.

Most people neglect to take this step. They fail to make notes regarding their need for input from other parties. Unfortunately, if their workflow depends on others, this omission will ruin their estimates concerning the time needed to complete tasks. They'll end up spending valuable time in limbo, waiting for other people to act. This, of course, will hobble their ability to get things done, severely impacting their productivity.

How To Maintain A Well-Oiled To-Do List System

Your master task list, context lists, and daily to-do lists are components of a broader system. Their effectiveness depends on that system's integrity.

If you have a well-oiled system in place, your lists will help you to get important work done faster and with more efficiency. If your system is faulty, your lists can actually hurt your workflow, sabotage your time management, and demolish your productivity.

In the following sections, I'll show you, step by step, how to maintain an effective to-do list system. Most of these tips build upon core concepts we've already covered in previous sections. A few introduce new concepts. All of them are essential to creating a system that guarantees your to-do lists help you to get your important work done.

Tip #1: Keep A "Tiny Task" Batch List

I mentioned the use of a batch list in Step #5 of the section *How To Create The Perfect To-Do List*. The purpose of a batch list is to organize all of your tiny tasks in one place. Tiny tasks are items that take less than 10 minutes to complete. The idea is to batch them together and address them during a single work session.

Tiny tasks don't belong on your daily to-do list. Remember, your daily list should be limited to seven items. Save the space for high-value tasks that require more time to complete (a minimum of 15 minutes).

Nor should tiny tasks remain on your master list. They'll just end up cluttering it.

Instead, place them on a separate batch list. When you have extra time, choose a few to work on. Cross the items off your list as you complete them.

Following are examples of tiny tasks that belong on a separate batch list:

- Make the bed
- Start a load of laundry
- Email client
- Record yesterday's sales data
- Empty the dishwasher
- Schedule a meeting with coworker
- Make a dinner reservation
- Check voicemail
- Take out the trash
- Update the boss on an ongoing project
- Return a phone call
- Declutter your workstation
- Pay bills online
- Update software

Each of these tasks can be completed in a few minutes. The problem is, when you address them sporadically throughout your day, you risk them becoming distractions. They'll interrupt your workflow, derailing your momentum and destroying your creativity.

They'll tempt you to multitask, which will introduce task switching costs. Switching costs negatively impact your performance and cause your productivity to plummet.

The solution is simple. Batch these tiny tasks together. Set aside 30 to 45 minutes to work on them. This will allow you to focus on the items, one by one, without distracting you from your important work. You'll have set aside a separate work session to address them.

Whenever possible, batch together tasks that are related by context. For example, if you need to return several emails, treat each one as a separate to-do item and handle all of them during a single batch session. Likewise, if you need to do several chores at home, batch them together and address them at the same time.

Working on related to-do items minimizes switching costs. As a result, you'll get more done in less time and make fewer errors along the way.

Tip #2: Remain Vigilant Against Feeling Overwhelmed

One of the biggest threats to any task management system is the feeling of overwhelm.

You've no doubt experienced it at some point. For example, you've checked your email and become discouraged after seeing hundreds of messages sitting in your inbox. You've looked at your master to-do list and become disheartened by its length and lack of task-level context. You've looked at your daily to-do list and become demoralized after discovering the items you've included are vague projects rather than actionable tasks.

The good news is that you can eliminate - or at least minimize - these problems by implementing the steps we covered in the section

How To Create The Perfect To-Do List. A solid to-do list system will help you to efficiently manage your workload.

But the threat of feeling overwhelmed will always be present. If it gains a foothold in your mind, it will siphon your enthusiasm, extinguish your motivation, and block your creativity.

For these reasons, it's imperative that you remain vigilant against it. You must always be on your guard. Circumstances will conspire to make you feel overloaded with work. For example, your boss may foist more and more responsibilities onto your shoulders. Your coworkers might attempt to delegate their to-do items to you. Your spouse may add to your growing list of obligations without realizing that you lack the bandwidth to handle them in a timely manner.

Your to-do lists will help you in this regard. Assuming you're creating lists as described in the section *How To Create The Perfect To-Do List*, you'll be able to gauge your availability and take on new tasks - or deflect them - accordingly.

Don't underestimate the demotivating power of feeling overwhelmed. It will raise your stress levels, make you more susceptible to distractions, and prevent you from getting important stuff done.

Tip #3: Define Your To-Do Lists By Context

We've covered this concept in detail already. But it bears repeating as we explore how to create and maintain an effective to-do list system.

In Step #6 of the section *How To Create The Perfect To-Do List*, I mentioned that every task on your master list should be accompanied by contextual details. For example, you should specify the project with which the task is associated; the type of activity (analytical, creative, etc.); and whether there are any location-based constraints attached to it.

Noting these details may, at first, seem like a waste of time. But they're crucial to sustaining a smoothly-operating to-do list system. When you add context to the tasks on your master list, you can quickly identify the ones you should work on.

For example, suppose you're responsible for a high-priority project that has a looming deadline. You would focus on the tasks that move that project forward (project-based context).

Or suppose it's mid-afternoon and your energy levels are low. You'd do well to focus on mindless work (e.g. data entry, decluttering your desk, etc.) rather than analytical or creative work (activity-based context).

Or suppose you're at the office. You would focus on to-do items that can only be done there (location-based context).

Task-level context informs your decisions regarding what you should do next. While providing contextual details upfront takes time, doing so streamlines the decision-making process later. It's a good investment.

I recommended earlier that you maintain multiple lists by context. This is an approach that works for me. I suspect it will work for you as long as you apply it with consistency.

Tip #4: Conduct Weekly Reviews

Weekly reviews are critical. They make the difference between a system that motivates you to get important stuff done and one that encourages you to procrastinate. They determine whether you successfully keep track of everything you need to do or let items fall through the cracks.

Most people neglect to conduct regularly-scheduled reviews. They think them unnecessary. They assume they have a solid grasp of their workload, and thus formal reviews would be a waste of time.

This may indeed be the case for you. Suppose your master list has fewer than a dozen items on it. You can probably keep track of everything without conducting weekly reviews.

But chances are, you have far more than a dozen tasks to monitor. If you have any responsibilities or goals at all, your master list is sure to grow past the point of being manageable without periodic review sessions. Count on it.

Imagine that your to-do list has more than 100 items on it. Without periodic reviews, you won't be able to accurately gauge your progress on them. Nor will you be able to mentally organize them according to context. It's too much to keep track of.

This is the purpose of holding a weekly review session. It gives you an opportunity to evaluate the extent of your progress toward your various goals. It also gives you a chance to reprioritize tasks as needed.

I conduct my weekly reviews on Sunday evenings. You should choose a day and time that accommodates your circumstances. Note that you'll need to focus. So, set aside 45 minutes during which you can work undisturbed.

How do you conduct a weekly review? Here are the basic steps:

1. Gather all of your to-do lists. This includes your master list and context-based lists.

2. Do a brain dump of all the tasks and projects floating around your head. Add them to your master list.

3. Break down new projects into individual tasks.

4. Separate new tasks according to context (project, type, and location). Create new context-based lists, if necessary.

5. Clear out your email inbox. Send responses if they're necessary. If an email requires you to take action, but isn't urgent, make a note of it on your master to-do list and archive the message. Also, archive emails that don't warrant a response or action, but may be needed later. Delete the rest.

6. Review your master list and context-based lists. Purge tasks that are no longer necessary or important.

7. Note the tasks that are both important and urgent. Mark them as candidates for your daily to-do list.

8. Note the tasks for which you're waiting on input from others. Write down the person's name and the date you expect to receive his or her input. The date will tell you when to follow up if you don't receive it.

9. Review your current deadlines for high-value tasks. Make adjustments if necessary.

10. Assign deadlines to new tasks you've added to your master list and context-based lists.

11. Review your calendar for the coming week. Create your daily to-do list based on your availability.

The above may seem like a lot of work. In truth, it is. But it's a good investment. A weekly review is integral to maintaining a well-oiled to-do list system. It will ensure you focus your limited time on the high-value items that will move forward the work that is most important to you.

Tip #5: Update Your List Of Goals

Your goals dictate how you spend your time. They give you clarity about what you want to achieve, in the short run as well as years down the road.

They make you accountable. When you know what you're trying to achieve, you become aware that every decision you make either moves you closer toward your goals or further away from them.

Goals also help you to focus on what's important. In Step #2 of the section *How To Create The Perfect To-Do List*, I recommended assigning a specific goal to each task on your list. The purpose of doing so is to give yourself an incentive to act. When you know the reason a particular task needs to be done, and the reason is consistent with something you want to accomplish, you'll develop laser-sharp focus on the task. You'll treat it as a priority.

First, create goals that are specific. Most people's goals are vague. That's a problem because, without specifics, it's difficult to gauge one's progress toward achieving them.

Take a look at the following example.

Vague goal: retire early.

Specific goal: retire by your 60th birthday with $2 million in liquid investments and a $5,000 monthly income.

Note how the vague version makes it nearly impossible to track your progress. There's no way to tell how close you are to achieving it because you haven't clearly defined the metrics by which you gauge success.

In contrast, the specific version provides trackable metrics.

Second, write down your goals. You'll be less likely to abandon them.

In 1979, graduates of Harvard's MBA program were asked whether they wrote down their goals. Eighty-four percent admitted they had no specific goals; thirteen percent claimed they had goals, but had not written them down; three percent wrote down their goals along with their plans to achieve them.

In 1989, the interviewers followed up with the graduates. They noted two remarkable findings. First, the 13% who had goals earned more than the 84% who had no goals. Second, the 3% who wrote down their goals earned 10 times as much as the 97% who did not write them down.

You can see there's power in committing your goals to paper.

To recap, you've created goals that are specific. And you've written them down.

Now what?

The third step is to review them monthly. Set aside 30 minutes at the end of each month to track your progress and reevaluate whether any of your goals have changed. If they have, make notes accordingly.

Your to-do list system is driven by the things you want to accomplish in your life. Some of your goals will be short-term in nature - for example, you might want to earn a promotion at work this year. Others will be long-term in nature - for example, retiring by the age of 60 with $2 million in liquid investments.

Review and update your goals each month. Doing so will help keep your to-do list system running smoothly.

Tip #6: Avoid Getting Bogged Down In Methodology

It's common for people interested in being more productive and learning how to better manage their time to try numerous systems. We discussed some of those systems as they relate specifically to to-do lists in the section *10 Most Popular To-Do List Systems*. When we broaden the spectrum to include systems related to time management in general, we encounter the Pomodoro Technique, timeboxing, the Franklin-Covey system, Zen To Done, and others.

Trying different systems is important. It's the only way to determine which ones complement the way you work. It's also a great way to discover individual tactics you can include in your own approach.

This is essentially what we've done in this action guide; we explored several of the top to-do list methodologies with an eye for the features that seem to hold the most value. We then created a to-do list system using some of those features.

But there's a dark side to productivity and time management systems: it's easy to get bogged down in them. We become so focused on the methodologies created to help us manage our time that they begin to negatively impact our productivity. This is a version of the problem we discussed in the section *The Productivity Paradox: How Your To-Do Lists Are Hampering Your Success*. The systems designed to help us end up holding us back.

The purpose of any productivity system, including your to-do list system, is to help you get the right things done on time. The goal is to increase your efficiency and ultimately make your life easier to manage.

When you focus on methodologies to the point that they become the priority, you risk forfeiting these goals.

You probably know someone who fits this description. She adopts every new time management system she comes across. Or she uses a system that is so complex and requires so much time to maintain that it ends up hampering her productivity. (To see examples, visit YouTube and search for "time management binder systems.")

Your to-do list system is there to support you. It's there to help you get the important stuff done and move you closer to your goals. It's not there to rule your life.

Don't become so bogged down in the methodology that you forget its purpose. Be open to modifying aspects of your to-do list system as your needs change. Be willing to adopt new features as you discover better, more efficient, ways of doing things.

Just remember your to-do list system is there to aid you, not control you.

Tip #7: Build And Follow A System That Works For YOU

There is no perfect to-do list system. The approach that works for others may not work as well for you. This is a point I've stressed throughout this action guide.

While the basic building blocks of an effective system - e.g. deadlines, task-level context, and separation of current and future tasks - have universal value, other aspects are less crucial. They can be modified or swapped out for others.

In fact, you *should* modify or swap them out if doing so improves your ability to get things done.

The aim of this action guide is not to force you to work within the constraints of a single system. On the contrary, its aim is to help you to create a system that works for *you*.

Note our progress thus far...

We discussed the most popular to-do list strategies used today, highlighting their best features. We also covered the fundamentals of effective lists, all of which are vital to creating a successful system. And we're now discussing the core features of a solid support structure that will ensure your system works smoothly over the long run.

The concepts we've covered have had a single goal: to help you create your personal to-do list system, a methodology that works for you. Your approach is going to look different than my approach. That's as it should be. Our circumstances are different. Our work processes are different. Our predilections and proclivities are different.

It follows that our respective to-do list systems will be different.

It's worth repeating that the basic building blocks, covered in the section *How To Create The Perfect To-Do List*, are the same. They're essential to creating an effective system. But your application of them will differ from mine.

The most important thing is that your approach complements *your* workflow and circumstances.

Tip #8: Be Consistent

Your to-do list system will only be as effective as the consistency with which you apply the principles we've discussed in this action guide. Consistency is the key to success in any endeavor, and maintaining a successful task management system is no exception.

It's one thing to know how to create effective to-do lists. It's another thing entirely to apply the basics on a daily basis. Doing the latter will mean the difference between a smoothly-operating system and one that eventually overwhelms you.

The challenge is twofold. First, consistency requires habit change. Left to our own devices, most of us are inclined to give ourselves too much latitude. We need to build the habit of taking action on a regular basis. It doesn't come naturally to us.

The second challenge is that skipping a day or two can have a snowball effect. Once you skip a day, it becomes easier to skip forthcoming days.

You can probably relate to this from experience. Ever notice how postponing an unpleasant activity - for example, visiting the dentist - makes it easier to postpone that activity again and again? The same thing can happen if you fail to apply the steps and tips explained in this action guide with consistency.

If you struggle with being consistent, I recommend you use the "Jerry Seinfeld" strategy. Here's how it works (I'll explain its history in a moment):

First, learn the 10 steps to creating an effective to-do list system. (These steps were explained in detail in the section titled *How To Create The Perfect To-Do List*.)

Second, memorize the eight tips for ensuring your system runs smoothly over the long run. (These eight tips are found in the current section titled *How to Maintain A Well-Oiled To-Do List System*.)

Third, buy a wall calendar that displays the entire year on a single sheet. Also, buy a red pen.

Lastly, apply the steps and tips you've learned to your master list, context-based lists, and daily to-do lists each day. After you've successfully done so, cross the day off with the red pen.

Seinfeld used this strategy when he was on the comedy club circuit. He would write jokes each day, crossing the day off on his calendar. The red "X" marks eventually formed a chain, which he made certain to never break. Seinfeld credited this "chain" strategy, which encouraged him to write consistently, to becoming a skilled comedian.

Until you develop the habit of consistent execution, try Seinfeld's approach. I used it to train myself to exercise. It worked perfectly. I'd be willing to bet you'll have similar success using it to maintain your to-do list system.

What To Do If You Fall Off The Wagon

In the previous section, I noted that you must be consistent with your to-do list system if you want it to be effective. The problem is, being consistent, day after day, is difficult. It's tempting to let things slip here and there.

Unfortunately, letting things slip can quickly lead to a spiral of decline. Before you know it, your system has crumbled and you're trying to dig yourself out from under it.

This is more common than you might imagine. Many people fall off the productivity wagon. They let their systems collapse around them, even though doing so carries a considerable cost.

Why does this happen? It happens because any productivity system, whether it's focused on task management or workflow efficiency, is a series of learned behaviors. Keeping it running smoothly requires developing new habits and applying them with consistency. It takes commitment and resilience.

Expect to face challenges as you work to keep your to-do list system running smoothly. There will be times when you feel like throwing in the towel. That's understandable. Replacing bad habits with good ones is tough work.

The key is what you choose to do when you stumble.

Some people give up. They figure it's too difficult to maintain their to-do list systems, and point to their failure to successfully keep them going as evidence. With a defeatist attitude, they let their systems crumble and surrender to the consequences.

Others take the opposite approach. They acknowledge that perfection is a pipe dream. A delusion. They expect to stumble occasionally. Instead of giving up, however, they forgive themselves and get back in the proverbial saddle.

I encourage you to take this latter approach if, or when, you stumble. Don't beat yourself up; self-guilt has no value. Instead, brush the dust off and forgive yourself.

Then, try to determine the reason you stumbled. Was it a lack of clarity regarding some aspect of your to-do list system? Was it a lack of energy that induced you to neglect your weekly reviews? Are you trying to do too much given the limited amount of time at your disposal?

Once you know the reason (or reasons) for your slip-up, you can make changes to correct the underlying problem.

A properly-developed and consistently-executed to-do list system will improve your productivity as well as your quality of life. You'll experience less stress and enjoy more free time to connect with those whom you love. You'll also enjoy more freedom to pursue personal interests.

But it's important to realize you'll encounter challenges. What you do in the face of these challenges will determine whether your system does its job over the long run.

Offline vs. Online: Where Should You Create Your To-Do Lists?

It's the debate that never seems to end.

Should you use digital tools to create and organize your to-do lists or plain 'ole pen and paper?

The truth is, there's no universally-correct answer. There are pros and cons to both methods. This section will present the cases for both sides, so you can choose the option that's right for you.

The Case For Pen And Paper

It's not sexy. But millions of people swear by its effectiveness. The truth is, there's a lot to like about creating your to-do lists on paper.

First, there's something about writing down a task that cements it in our minds. We're more likely to remember it. We're also more inclined to act on it. Typing the words on your laptop or phone has a lesser effect. This is one of the reasons I recommended writing down your goals (in the section *How To Maintain A Well-Oiled To-Do List System*).

Second, a notepad will adapt seamlessly to your preferred method of jotting down notes. It's perfect for linear organization, the format used for a typical to-do list. It can also handle mind-mapping and other note-taking styles.

Third, you can avoid worrying about yet another piece of software. Chances are, you already use a number of applications, from word processors to spreadsheets, throughout your day. Any of them could potentially fail, interrupting your workflow and destroying your momentum.

That's the downside of relying on software.

It's worth noting that using cloud-based apps doesn't guarantee round-the-clock access. What happens if the servers go down, are hacked, or you don't have access to your laptop or phone?

These problems are irrelevant - at least in terms of task management - when you use pen and paper to maintain your to-do lists.

Fourth, a notepad is easy to carry. You can keep it with you at all times, jotting to-do items down as you think of them. Using a digital tool is higher maintenance. For example, consider the challenge of keeping track of tasks on a laptop. Whenever you think of a new item, you have to retrieve and fire up your laptop, navigate to your task management software (or website, if the software is in the cloud), and type things out. Using your phone isn't much easier.

Fifth, there's nothing like the tactile experience of using a pen to cross off a completed to-do item. Clicking a button on your computer screen or phone won't give you the same feeling. It's not nearly as gratifying.

Let's now shift our focus and explore the reasons to use digital tools to create and maintain your to-do lists.

The Case For Keeping Your To-Do Lists Online

Digital solutions abound for those who want to maintain their task management systems online. From Todoist and Evernote to Trello and Asana, there's no shortage of apps with which to create and organize your to-do lists. And more apps are introduced each year.

In the previous section, I highlighted five reasons to use paper-based to-do lists. Here, I'll give you five reasons to use digital tools. Remember, the right approach is the one that works best for you.

The first reason to go digital is that today's apps make it very easy to organize your task lists by context. You'll recall from the section *How To Create The Perfect To-Do List* that you should maintain multiple lists organized by project, type of activity, and location. You might also have additional context-based lists. Organizing and maintaining them is simpler with tools like Todoist than doing so on paper.

Second, you can easily move to-do items from list to list. This is useful if you need to re-categorize tasks or make changes to the contextual details attached to them.

Third, many online apps like Todoist allow you to set alarms and reminders based on date and time. Imagine having a master task list with 200 items, each of which you've given a deadline. Now imagine the online app alerting you of impending deadlines so you can prioritize your daily to-do lists accordingly. You can't do that with paper-based lists.

Fourth, you can organize projects and tasks in a nested structure. This improves visualization of your workload. You can get a bird's-eye view of the tasks that make up larger projects and monitor your progress toward completing those projects.

Fifth, tools like Todoist allow you to integrate your to-do lists with your calendar. This is an important feature since your calendar defines your availability. Once you create your lists in Todoist, you can sync them to your calendar tool of choice (for example, Google Calendar). It's worth noting that integration with some calendars is dependent on third-party tools, such as Zapier and IFTTT (If This,

Then That). Don't worry. These tools are designed to be easy and simple to use.

So, should you use paper-based to-do lists or create and maintain your lists online? The answer depends on how you work. Some people thrive with paper. Personally, I prefer to use Todoist. It's easy to use, free (a premium account costs less than $30 per year), and platform-independent. You can use it on your laptop, iPhone, or Android device.

If you suspect a paper-based system won't suit your needs, I highly recommend Todoist. It's perfect for personal use.

If you manage projects and teams, try Trello. Like Todoist, it's free with a lot of useful features. You can upgrade to a premium account if the need arises.

How To Incorporate Your Calendar Into Your To-Do Lists

Another big standoff in the productivity space is between to-do lists and calendars. Is one option better than the other? Both have staunch advocates and vocal detractors.

The truth is, neither tool should be used to the exclusion of the other. The best way to maximize your output each day is to combine your to-do list and calendar.

I mentioned in the previous section that your calendar defines your availability. It tells you how much time you have at your disposal to work on to-do items. To that end, it does no good to create a to-do list that requires five hours of work if you only have three hours available to you. Doing so will set yourself up for failure. That, in turn, will lead to disappointment, stress, and frustration.

There's an easy way to avoid this outcome: sync your calendar and to-do lists. Let the former inform your decisions regarding the latter.

Here's a simple approach:

First, at the end of the day, review your calendar for the following day. Determine when you'll be in meetings, on conference calls, or otherwise unavailable.

Second, estimate how much time you'll be able to allocate to your to-do items. Don't forget to leave yourself time for lunch and breaks. Also, pad the estimate to accommodate unexpected delays - for example, impromptu requests for help from your boss and coworkers.

Second, build the following day's to-do list. You should have a fairly good idea regarding how long each task will take you to complete (recall step #8 from the section *How To Create The Perfect To-Do List*). Create your to-do list based on your availability.

Third, think of your day as a series of 30-minute time chunks. An hour-long meeting will require two chunks. A two-hour conference call will require four chunks. These periods should be blocked off on your calendar.

Fourth, schedule time to work on your to-do items during the periods that are not blocked off.

For example, suppose this is your schedule for tomorrow:

- 8:00 a.m. to 9:00 a.m. - Meeting with your boss
- 10:30 a.m. to noon - Conference call with sales team
- Noon to 1:00 p.m. - Lunch
- 3:00 p.m. to 3:30 p.m. - Department meeting

The above schedule reveals the periods during which you'll be available to work through your to-do list:

- 9:00 a.m. to 10:30 a.m.
- 1:00 p.m. to 3:00 p.m.
- 3:30 p.m. to 5:00 p.m.

That's five and a half hours. Trim 45 minutes for breaks and impromptu requests, and you're left with four hours and 45 minutes. You can now create a realistic to-do list for tomorrow based on your availability.

Your to-do list is an inventory of what you hope to accomplish during the course of a given day. Your calendar determines whether it's possible. Working with one tool, but not the other, is a recipe for failure. Use them both to manage your time effectively and set reasonable, realistic daily productivity goals.

What Is A "Done List"
(And Should You Keep One?)

One of the most common challenges to staying productive over the long run is a lack of motivation. You know the feeling. You run around all day to get things done only to wonder at the end of the day "where the heck did I spend my time?"

Everyone goes through this. Everyone experiences this feeling from time to time. Many experience it on a regular basis.

The results are predictable: frustration, stress, and guilt for failing to complete important, high-value tasks.

A "done list" seeks to fix this problem. It records all of the tasks you accomplish throughout the day. The idea is that seeing the completed tasks will inspire you to get more done. The done list rejuvenates you, filling you with the motivation you need to press onward.

So, does it work? Can a done list actually motivate you to take action?

It depends. If you need motivation to work on tasks, this can be a sound strategy. Your done list will highlight your accomplishments during the day and ensure that you don't forget about them. In contrast, when you work from a to-do list, crossing off tasks as you complete them, it's easy to overlook how much you've actually gotten done.

On the other hand, if you don't need motivation to take action, a done list may be unnecessary. In fact, it may even hurt your productivity since it's another list for you to manage. It will needlessly encumber your to-do list system.

If you're not sure whether a done list will help you to get things done, I recommend that you experiment with it. Maintain a done list for two weeks and note how it influences you. If you discover that it has a positive impact on your productivity, keep using it. Otherwise, drop it. Remember, the point of this entire action guide is to create a to-do list system that works for *you*.

In the next section, I'll explain how to create a done list. It's drop-dead simple.

How To Create A "Done List"

First, your done list should not replace your to-do list. I mention this because many proponents of done lists recommend doing exactly that. They advise abandoning your to-do lists entirely.

I disagree with that position 100%.

It should be clear that I feel an effective to-do list system is invaluable to organizing tasks and projects and getting things done. A done list cannot possibly take its place as a task management strategy. It's not sufficiently flexible.

That said, it can be a useful part of your to-do list system if you're motivated by seeing your daily accomplishments. So here's how to create and make use of a done list.

First, write down every task you complete during the course of your day. The size of the task doesn't matter. Nor does its priority. Did you deliver the report your boss tasked you with last week? Write it down. Did you schedule a meeting with your managers? Make a note of it. Did you follow up with a prospective client regarding your bid for a new project? If so, put it on your done list!

Second, review your done list after you've officially called it a day.

Take notice of how much you've accomplished. Then, take the time to appreciate your hard work. Give yourself a pat on the back.

Third, the following morning, before you tackle the new day's to-do list, look at yesterday's done list. Note again how many tasks you completed. Use this as motivation to be just as productive during the current day.

That's it. That's your done list in action.

I don't use a done list. That's not because the practice is ineffective. On the contrary, many people find it to be highly effective. I've tried it and found it does little for me.

As I mentioned, if a motivational boost prompts you to work more efficiently, experiment with using a done list. You may find it adds significant value to your workflow. Just don't let it replace your to-do list system.

Final Thoughts On Creating Effective To-Do Lists

I've mentioned this point a few times throughout this action guide, but it's worth repeating one last time: your to-do list system should complement your workflow. It should suit your method of getting things done.

I've given you the basic ingredients in this guide. I've also highlighted important features that should be a part of your system.

But ultimately, the task management strategy you design for yourself should be tailored in a way that works for *you*.

Here's another point that bears repeating: the purpose of your task lists - from your master task list to your daily to-do lists - isn't to make sure you get everything done. Rather, their purpose is to make sure you're focusing your limited time and attention on your most important work.

Remember, being productive isn't about keeping yourself busy. It's about getting the right things done based on your short and long-term goals.

One of the biggest advantages of the to-do list formula I've described in this action guide is that it allows you to get everything out of your head. You can dump everything onto paper or into an online solution like Todoist). From there, you can categorize items by context, deadlines, and other details. This ensures important work floats to the top while simultaneously preventing lower-priority items from falling through the cracks.

Lastly, once you've created a sound system, the most important thing you can do is to consistently apply the basic principles. Do so day after day without fail. Consistency is the oil that keeps the engine running.

You have a million things to do today (not to mention tomorrow, next week, and next month). It's not possible to remember all of them. Nor is it possible to organize them effectively in your head.

The solution is to make to-do lists.

You now have the recipe for creating to-do lists that work. You also know how they fit within the framework of a broader task management system. Armed with this insight, you can now create lists that will guarantee you get the important stuff in your life done!

May I Ask You A Small Favor?

I'd like to thank you for taking the time to read this action guide. It means the world to me. I know there are numerous books available on the subject. I'm honored that you chose to spend this time reading my book.

As you know, I'm an independent author. That being the case, one of my biggest priorities is to spread the word about my action guides.

If you enjoyed reading *To-Do List Formula: A Stress-Free Guide To Creating To-Do Lists That Work!*, would you consider letting others know about it? There are several ways you can do so. For example, you could:

1. Leave a review on Amazon
2. Leave a review at Goodreads.com
3. Tell folks about it on your blog
4. Share it on Facebook or Twitter
5. Mention it to your friends and family members

Reviews on Amazon encourage other readers to give independent authors like myself a chance. They help more than I can describe. And believe me, I can use all the help I get.

Thanks again for taking the time to read *To-Do List Formula: A Stress-Free Guide To Creating To-Do Lists That Work!* I sincerely appreciate it.

If you'd like to be notified when I release new action guides (typically at a steep discount), please sign up for my mailing list at http://artofproductivity.com/free-gift/. You'll receive a free PDF copy of my 40-page guide *Catapult Your Productivity: The Top 10 Habits You Must Develop To Get More Things Done.* You'll also receive periodic tips, tricks, and hacks for managing your time and designing an enriching, fully-satisfying lifestyle.

All the best,
Damon Zahariades
http://artofproductivity.com

Other Productivity Action Guides by Damon Zahariades

The 30-Day Productivity Plan: Break The 30 Bad Habits That Are Sabotaging Your Time Management - One Day At A Time!
This action guide will help you to identify and break the bad habits that are preventing you from achieving your goals. Organized into 30 easy-to-read daily chapters, it's filled with hundreds of actionable tips.

* * *

Digital Detox: Unplug To Reclaim Your Life
Stress levels are rising. Relationships are suffering. Our phones and other devices are largely to blame. Digital Detox provides a step-by-step blueprint for people who want to take a break from technology and enjoy life unplugged.

* * *

The Time Chunking Method: A 10-Step Action Plan For Increasing Your Productivity
The Time Chunking Method is one of the most popular time management strategies in use today. If you struggle with getting things done, you need this action guide. Productivity experts around the world attest to the method's effectiveness!

* * *

To-Do List Formula: A Stress-Free Guide To Creating To-Do Lists That Work!

Most people use to-do lists that hamper their productivity and leave them with unfinished tasks. This action guide highlights the reasons and shows you how to create effective to-do lists that guarantee you get your important work done!

For a complete list, please visit
http://artofproductivity.com/my-books/